From the Shallow End to the Deep End

Ninety-Five Sonnets

AJ Streator

© 2025 AJ Streator, LLC. All Rights Reserved.

All rights reserved. No part of this book may be reproduced without written permission of the Copyright owner or publisher.
For more information, please contact:
ajstreator@ajstreator.com

ISBN: 979-8-9942696-1-9

Book cover art by Jocelyn VanFleet

Illustrations by Jocelyn VanFleet

Copy editing by AdCo Agency

Published by AJ Streator

This Book
Is Dedicated To

**My Mother
and to
My Children**

Navigating the Sonnets' Waters

Introduction -- vii

Prologue --- ix

The Shallow End --- 01

Middle of the Pool -------------------------------------- 48

The Deep End -- 95

Epilogue -- xcvi

"For them, the pool was far too small to think;
For us, it wasn't deep enough to sink."

AJ Streator

Introduction and Acknowledgements

A long time ago in a high school language arts course, a teacher challenged students in the room to discover an unknown contemporary author and introduce that author's work to the class. I secretly wrote my own poem, printed it and made it look "fancy," and presented it to the class under a pseudonym. On that day, AJ Streator was born.

Decades later I find myself engulfed in a jealous career that has little use for poetry, yet I still possess volumes of unpublished, unknown, and unread material created in my "spare" time. It took an unexpected life experience, something that catapulted me into my "Darkest Times," to inspire and motivate the multi-year journey and manifestation of poetry into this collection. One of my goals was to create something different with this compilation, so I selected the traditional structure of the Shakespearean sonnet, but crafted much of the verse around complex circumstances often examined under more contemporary formats.

If I try to acknowledge and thank everyone who provided inspiration for the sonnets in this collection, I will no doubt omit important people. Know that if you have been a part of my life you will see yourself somewhere in these stanzas, and I thank you profoundly for helping shape the poet I have become. Whether or not you are an intimate part of these sonnets, I hope that somewhere in these pages the poetry can convey upon you a portion of the passion that was put into them.

Prologue

Bright Suns Rising

When clouds assemble, skies refuse to clear
as shadows hide an unsuspecting day;
Hold fast that hope will vanquish what you fear
and light a path to set you on your way.
A sorrowed heart as burdened as it be
holds sparks of joy within its darkest hour;
through silver threads that only you can see,
revealing that each dawn distributes power.
Strength can rise from silent winds inbound,
just as rising suns subdue a frost;
In darkness, streaks of beauty can be found
as love survives the moments seeming lost.
Turn your dreams to where bright lights might shine
and let your heart unfold to stay divine.

Sonnet No. 1

The Shallow End

Hardly old enough to read a clock
but far enough away to hide his call;
The small boy started fishing from a dock
and no one in his family eyed his fall.
A teenage hero saw him from afar
as brothers played and parents sipped their drinks;
the gallant stranger hastened insofar
with very little time to stop and think.

The champion saved the little boy that day
but never spoke again what he had done;
Too ashamed his parents were to say
what tragedy converged upon their son.
Older now, the little lad must look
deep inside himself to write his book.

Sonnet No. 2

Simpler Times

We didn't have much money young of age.
We didn't know the difference anyway;
the furnace worked and music was our rage
and evening was a time we chose to stay.
We didn't travel on vacation trips
as there was much that we could not afford;
we learned to labor hard and count our tips
and very seldom found that we were bored.
As we grew, we listened to them teach
disparities in economic class;
we set our sights on different heights to reach
and rise above the contrast in the mass.
    I wish today my questions seemed as clear
    and I could find the answers just as near.

Sonnet No. 3

Dear Santa

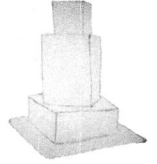

This year please care for the little ones;
Let them all be thankful for the season;
Help them rise and see the morning sun
and learn of Baby Jesus and His reason.
Also bring your comfort to the older;
Give them solemn joy in later years;
help their faith develop even bolder.

If alone, please wipe away their tears.

Rid this world of needless hate and hunger;
Grant our leaders wisdom in their choices;
This for both the dying and the younger;
valor meant to hear each others' voices.

If by chance you've something left to send,
I could really use another friend.

Sonnet No. 4

Mother Dearest

Unique in every way for sons eternal
fate defied the kingdom with our Mother
to play all parts and be all hands maternal.
I know there never could have been another.
The fortunes could not bless us with a sister;
knowledge shunned us for that dreadful call
in our kingdom all were known as mister;
we suffered what was lacking through it all
but steadfast Mother, always there she stood
a lantern shedding sunlight from her shelf,
reminding us of all that's just and good
and never thinking first about herself.
The kingdom's gone, the monarch overrun
but she will always have her grateful sons.

Sonnet No. 5

Ice And Betts And I

We were best of friends when we were seven.
Ice and Betts and I made quite a run;
we barely spoke beyond our age eleven
when our reign as kings was overrun.

Ice was tough and fearsome in a jam;
no one took his challenge to a duel.
One day Ice made fun of who I am
so I beat him up right after school.
Betts was reared by a more important dad
he had the biggest house and nicest clothes.
When his family lost all that they had,
Betts moved to a town his mother chose.

We rarely keep our friends from such an age,
sad it is when childhood turns its page.

Sonnet No. 6

The Constable

My mother's father was a famous cop.
From a mounted horse he sought the truth;
his disposition kept him from the top
but all the town knew not a better sleuth.
He weaved a labyrinth within his life,
failing most attempts to win his wealth
with toxic thoughts beyond his second wife
he lasted many years with guarded health.

His children carried deep disdain for him;
we didn't tell them of the times we met
but he was deeply hurt by their chagrin
and often spoke to me of his regrets.
I wish his children could have shed the shroud
and shared his legacy to make us proud.

Sonnet No. 7

Eyes Of A Child

Through hallowed gates we venture holding hands
where laughter lands on every welcome breeze;
from sprawling rides to savory hotdog stands
and all the games with prizes aimed to please.
Children's eyes grow wild and take the lead;
little girl's giggles fill with cheers
we chase the thrills but pause at times we need
to feed ourselves and vanquish all our fears.
The sun fades low but not the park's allure.
Massive lights ignite the colors bright.
Soon we tire with memories secure
and slowly leave to slumber for the night.
Children smile as lives are at their best,
And now they lay in bed to finally rest.

Sonnet No. 8

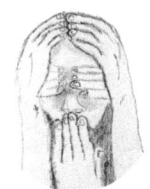

**Echoes From
A Different Room**

Look where bearcats, chiefs and eagles stray;
two brothers danced with stories to be told;
both had put their prowess on display;
one a rock, the other hands of gold.
One stood at the center of the line
he cleared a path like motorcades of steel.
The other took the end and chose to shine
ensuring every pass and run was real.

Which was better, the one who patterned deep
and often tallied points when taking flight,
or the other snapping from the keep
while moving mountains using all his might?

The verdict's clear, their parents win the prize
for raising two such legendary guys.

Sonnet No. 9

Resurrection

I played the game when uniforms were smaller.
Today the rules have changed and so have I.
I would have done it differently if taller,
instead I played the way they bid me try.
Coaches wouldn't listen to my plea
as I was just a boy but they were men
at the time they wouldn't talk to me;
I never cared enough to try again.

Now my youngest son pursues the game.
His skills are far beyond what I once knew;
I hope his coaches care to know his name
and act mature enough to talk it through.
With the many talents that he holds,
his passion brings me back into the fold.

Sonnet No. 10

Art (Hypo)Critics

Provocation sometimes is a calling
away from lessons begging that we teach;
Some will take their stage afraid of falling;
Others never see their heights to reach;
Critics self-proclaim their good intentions
while politics and money pave their way,
rather than to celebrate inventions
listening to messages conveyed.

Let irony reflect on only them;
Shallowness of thought should never sway
the inspirations growing from within
that show us what our artists have to say.
Encourage all to demonstrate their skill
and overcome misgivings in their will.

Sonnet No. 11

First Love

As juveniles we gazed across the room,
twirling heads each time our eyes would greet;
wondering what ahead of us might loom
and if our inner hearts would ever meet.
Youth did pass, we danced around with others
but I believed our lives would someday link;
even when you brought me to your mother
we never seemed to catch ourselves in sync.
Moments added miles between our thoughts;
I still believed we shared what you were dreading.
My songs and notes sent nothing that you sought,
and you joined with another at your wedding.
    Do you recall, and do you still agree,
    A gallant effort is half a victory?

Sonnet No. 12

Shifting
The Space - Time Vortex

Special moments complicate our lives
when unexpected heroes show their face
without an explanation that contrives
the destiny that scrambles into place.

A grade school teacher singles out a name
segregating from a settled class;
Life from there shall never be the same
Soaring high above the student mass.
An incongruous path falls into sight.
A seed for ingenuity is born.
Peculiar aspirations come to light;
a future once in doubt becomes adorned.

When life is drowned in darkness search for light
and when the daylight blinds you, seek the night.

Sonnet No. 13

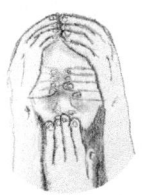

Father's Favorite Son

You were meant to pave the way for me
but you were gone, we barely spoke a word.
I came to know just why you had to flee;
the pain was all the same when I came third.
Our father cried the day you moved away;
A rarity I only witnessed twice.
Ironic as it was I came to pray
but not for him, I made my sacrifice.
Words we never spoke until his wake;
He may have finally learned to talk to you
but still at times his stubbornness awakes
a fate our middle brother surely knew.
Much of what united us is dead
but faith may show us better days ahead.

Sonnet No. 14

Mr. Bill And Mr. Bob

Two coaches much revered despite the others
who didn't preach their politics or prayers.
Widely known a pair of battling brothers
believing they should play their finest players.
Simple men and branded Bill and Bob;
better seen by us as "Colt" and "Bear"
they never needed prompting for their job
and no one questioned whether they were there.
Old of school and of a different breed.
Never needing players' love or praise.
They won the games they needed to succeed
and prepared their teams for unexpected days.

Although they may not reach the hall of fame
their players know the legends of their name.

Sonnet No. 15

Lost Games

Childhood athletics cut us deep
with competition teaching what it can;
absorbing lessons we were meant to keep
and molding little boys into a man.
Sometimes memories fail to save the game
when searching sidelines finds an empty seat.
Even as the crowd might roar my name
the eyes I sought were those I could not meet.
Instead those nights were spent with other folks
no doubt providing joy and evening fun;
he likely laughed at all their same-old jokes
but never knowing if my team had won.

Those moments could have been for us to share,
but they were lost because he wasn't there.

Sonnet No. 16

Leaving Much Unheard

The worst of leaders walk in armor clad
to hide the simple virtues that they lack
and crucial lessons that were never had
in favor of a belt whip on the back.
They yearn to be considered as a knight.
The smiles on their faces such a fluke.
They never end the day with wrong or right;
they never leave us room for much rebuke.
At their end they fail to understand
why the room is not as it should be;
no crowds of worship standing hand-in-hand
or kissing skies while falling to their knees.
Those who live to speak the final word
depart our world leaving much unheard.

Sonnet No. 17

Holding Hands

I remember when I held your hand.
Your touch was meant to lead to something more;
we whispered we would seek a future grand
and carry on together evermore.
You seemed to be as hypnotized as I
and helped us understand what we had dreamed.
Our smiles together reached into the sky,
your laughter felt like everything it seemed.
But then our tempered passions parted ways
and visions shared began to slowly fade;
Our distance turned from hours into days
and paths we laid together had decayed.
When I released your hand I should have known
without you I might sometimes feel alone.

Sonnet No. 18

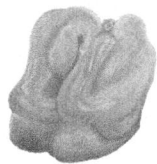

Brother's Keepers

Tell me how a childhood feels alone.
I shouldn't know from having older brothers
still I smelled a clean but empty home
awaiting me when leaving school with others.
My siblings fled when I was only eight
and I was given all their toys and clothes.
I had my choice of bedrooms, that was great
although I don't remember which I chose.

I would have liked to learn much more from them;
They understood what I was to endure.
Instead at any cost they did condemn
their former years to seek a cryptic cure.
My older wiser brothers were a pair
if only they remembered I was there.

Sonnet No. 19

Hollow Hearts
Leave Empty Thoughts

Together once we shaped our common goals
while others mocked we weathered every storm
then fate controlled and took its bitter tolls;
our ties unwound and spun a different form.
The paths we laid were slowly pulled apart
into a gorge too cavernous to cross
where common trust abandons hollow hearts;
a brother gone in fortune's winding toss.
Visions taste like echoes sounding clear
from days when faith and loyalty could grow;
now all is gone but sometimes very near
seem thoughts of places only we would go.
Still it hurts when evolution's day
means moments shared are forced to fade away.

Sonnet No. 20

Little Brother?

The little brother who I never had.
What wondrous plans our parents made for us
to conquer worlds while they were acting mad
and we had many puzzles to discuss.
Our futures rarely sounded blind or mute
but also never close enough to touch;
our artificial family in dispute
would somehow see us scatter in the clutch.
As we arose we couldn't much rely
and over time we sought our own rewards;
without a clear enlightened reason why
our paths diverged into a faint discord.
You're still a little brother near or far,
even when I wonder where you are.

Sonnet No. 21

Memorial Day

To understand the richness of this Day
which leaves a mystic impact on our lives;
where friends transcend upon a lake to play
and legends told will never reach our wives.
A group diverse as any one can be;
some are short while others tall and bold;
some were born into the family,
others since invited to the fold.
Some will dwell the land throughout the year
but only once does everyone attend;
On the day when everyone is near
and sworn we are to keep it to the end.
Come each Spring, to none of our dismay
we each await the next Memorial Day.

Sonnet No. 22

Soldier Boy Returns

Soldier Boy did travel far away;
his battle ground remains to us unknown.
Perhaps he crossed the line in Mandalay
or wore a mask to fight a despot's throne.
Everybody loved our Soldier Boy
and yearned that he return to us again;
he filled so many lives with hope and joy
and grew to lead the charge of many men.

Now Soldier Boy has travelled back to us.
We thank the Lord he rose above his wars
but Soldier Boy refuses to discuss
what happened to him when he left our shores.

Never mind the stories that we lack,
we celebrate that Soldier Boy is back.

Sonnet No. 23

The Girl From Kansas City

On a road trip with my oldest friend
in Kansas City to see another guy;
they wouldn't let their girlfriends attend,
we thought we'd give this weekend trip a try.
In a nightclub, girls are looking fine;
the others having fun surveying them
but none had any interest to be mine
and I was feeling like I'd been condemned.

Suddenly a tap upon my shoulder.
A lovely girl thought I might be her one;
finally, I had found my one beholder ...
but my friends decided we were done.
    Tragic that I never saw again
    this one who chose me over other men.

Sonnet No. 24

Illinois

In Illinois a golden harvest sways
beneath the vast and sprawling endless sky;
where Midwest charm is present every day
and gentle winds on rolling plains will lie.
Seasons change from summer warmth we know
to winter chills where snowflakes softly land;
in Spring the rivers rise and overflow
until the Autumn breaks with nature's hand.
People are the treasures in each town;
friendly neighbors tell their tales true.
Big and small, its cities never frown;
resurrecting how our frontier grew.
An earnest life where values still reside
and families live with peacefulness and pride.

Sonnet No. 25

By The Book

In Chapter One I wore my brothers' clothes;
I ate the lunch they gave me while at school.
I lived the history other people chose
while serving as their systematic fool.

Chapter Two revealed what to do.
I went to work in finely tailored suits
wasting wisdom someone thought I knew
while circling back to find my inner roots.

The tale turned in Chapters Three to Five;
Mistakes evolved to lessons that were learned.
I reinvented ways to stay alive
and illustrations changed as pages turned.

Just because we can't rewrite our prequel,
doesn't mean we can't improve our sequel.

Sonnet No. 26

Boys Do Cry

My father would be quite upset with me.
He believed no one should see men cry
at such times a man should turn and flee;
I never understood his reasons why.
Through his life I saw him weeping twice
because he felt too sorry for himself.
Pretending that I did not see his vice,
hoping that his whip stayed on its shelf.

Today I cry for friends, so call me weak.
Still I leave the room to hide my tears;
not because I see myself as meek
but teachings slowly fade throughout the years.
The philosophy at hand is not the same;
to cry for others does not carry shame.

Sonnet No. 27

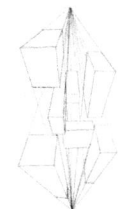

Election Day

This morning marks a new Election Day.
Some predict the most important ever;
I don't accept the tidings they convey
such as "we are in this thing together."
The news foretells for whom we should be fond
and who we should decide will be a crook.
They break the rules and think we might abscond
and pause to study how our options look.

Tomorrow will we have a brand new boss?
Will we all receive our new fair share?
Or will the trickle flow to save our loss
and tax us more than all of us can bare?
We'll seek the one who seems to care the most
but find the one who swings the greater votes.

Sonnet No. 28

Family Business

The family business - a treasure we must keep.
We watch some thrive and then embark to one
but don't assume it lends to better sleep
it captivates until each task is done.
Discover all its bounty start to end;
everything but never to relax;
Labors rise and beg your will to bend
and you can never forfeit to the tax.
If your inner drive can never find
fulfillment through machines or punching clocks
the path to overcome the daily grind
compels you to reject the clothes you mock.
The family business wagers on your skills
to find the reverence that your conscience wills.

Sonnet No. 29

Mother's Cure

Driving Mother to her doctor today.
She does this often as she's growing old;
in the car there's little left to say
other than the day is kind of cold.
She says she wants to leave the office quickly
although there's nothing else for her to do;
right now she isn't feeling very sickly
and days like these are growing rather few.

These trips allow us precious time together
to seize the passing moments of her phase
although we talk of little but the weather.
That's what Mother does to fill her days.
    If our journey fails to soothe her sorrow,
    we will do it all again tomorrow.

Sonnet No. 30

Planting A Legacy

In every child a seed sparks something new;
a path their own, unbound by others' past
when roots are shared as dreams start plowing through
to plot a different course but just as vast.

As parents hold their harvesting in sight,
younger sprouts will veer in other ways
to raise their destiny to brighter light
despite the change in weather's torrid days.
In what they seek, nothing is foretold
at times they must proceed to bloom alone;
but other's wisdom in the stories told
amplifies their journey as their own.

From children's hearts a destiny will sow
if we allow their inner strength to grow.

Sonnet No. 31

Call To Justice

Beyond the written words from history's hand,
lawyers stand with hearts of blazing steel
in statutes crafted by the law's command
unveiling to a world of great surreal.
With quills as swords and courtrooms their domain
both rhetoric and reason take their flight;
the demons of injustice must be slain
with all that's true and righteous still in sight.
Sacred written volumes beg to read;
such knowledge fuels a fair but vengeant flame
with eloquence of thought, their minds proceed
to seek a noble cause within the claim.
In our laws, a message they will find
the tools with which to benefit mankind.

Sonnet No. 32

Alfred, Lord Of Tension

Trouble lies where Alfred brings his wrath;
Never should he draw the tasks he holds.
His motives fuel the problems in his path
ignoring every answer as he scolds.
He clamors of the conflict's resolution,
facial vessels swell in scarlet red;
but never does he offer a solution
to backward clarity in what he said.
Does Alfred's ranting carry some regret
and will he understand when we are gone,
that he is part of all that he has met
and deference fades while leaders linger on?
The blackness of a callow man unfurled
is not the place to seek a newer world.

Sonnet No. 33

What Dreams Become

In bitter dreams with riches looming near
we yearn for signs of gold that slip away
with setting moons our hopes give way to fear
as empty pockets greet the rising day.
Human hands are ever strong and near
but never cleansing thoughts beyond dismay.
Paths will wind and wonder where to steer
while prospects pass with little left to say.

What triumph waits if coin is all to gain,
and tension gnaws where worries kneel low?
Ambition calls but fastens heavy chains
and often leaves an emptiness below.
Resolve the journey, strive to seize your way
and maybe fortune's end will find your day.

Sonnet No. 34

Sweetwater

Beneath the sky a river ties a bow,
Where two friends' dreams would never lay to rest;
Built on currents where passions always flow,
And wine and song will tip the water's crest.

Their hands grow stronger from the daily toil,
They shape their vision glowing in the shine;
And every special serving will embroil
Sparkles in the joy they hope you find.

The river whispers long into the night,
Of friendships forged in fires by the door;
And in the hearth the bistro's steadfast light
Assembles bonds that leave them wanting more.

Friends of Sweetwater know it will succeed,
In giving us a place we know we need.

Sonnet No. 35

Nat's Place

A quiet street where only weeds once grew,
Nat would build a Place born from her grace.
Through evening's labor to mornings' softened dew,
She broached her journey from this empty space.

Now it thrives like shooting stars in flight,
And night and day converge by her design;
Where once was just a dream now shimmers light,
And food and joy can always intertwine.

With every cup a story brews with care,
Into the warmth that fills each passing soul.
She pours her heart into the atmosphere,
A blend of peace and purpose is her goal.

The Place is here and now as patrons know;
A dream fulfilled in every cup aglow.

Sonnet No. 36

Junior

When the boy was born a choice was made
not to pass the echoes of my name.
During birth a brighter path was laid
undetermined by his family's claim.
No mirrored image binds his destiny,
nor weight of expectation's heavy chains.
His life, like mine, should lie in mystery
that lacks another's' bonds to bring him pain.
Names can brand like diction carved in stone
and clip his wings before they find the sky.
Let our children claim the lives they own
and they will choose the day they learn to fly.
Soon my son will soar and I will see
how he will shape his own identity.

Sonnet No. 37

Elysian Fields

On the field where youth and wisdom fight
to teach the game I can no longer play;
where every pitch and catch can strike delight
and build a memory as parents pray.
Eager eyes reflect a fearless flame.
Every cheer lets spirits rise and soar.
Win or lose, together in the game;
within their joy, I find my own once more.

The crack of bats ignites their pounding feet
and every play transcends a lesson bought.
'Tis a game where victories are sweet
but in defeat some character is taught.
Memories made from seasons that have flown
will never fade from children who have grown.

Sonnet No. 38

Power Of Three

My oldest has a step before his name.
Always quick to let me know it's there;
he's the first who thought he should disclaim
only to return to seek his share.

The middle one declares herself insane.
On many days I hesitate to see;
at least she doesn't hold me in disdain
even though we rarely can agree.

My youngest seems to be the most like me.
He often stumbles just the way I do;
will he be the closest of the three
or will there be a mission to pursue?

I hope one day they learn that they can be
a collective power far exceeding three.

Sonnet No. 39

Story Of
Fire And Light

A man of vision deep within his sight,
with bricks he piles his dedications high;
Invests so he may showcase all that might
give warmth throughout his lights that touch the sky.
His lanterns shine like stars above the ground;
each fire will spark the senses that will grow
and hearths will hum a gentle family sound.
Designs will find a friendly home to know.
With care he fills his kingly gleaming hall;
a haven for the best of us to gauge.
His name is loved, his craft is known to all
as life unfolds his everlasting stage.
In every room, creative lenses shout
the family dreams that never fade to doubt.

Sonnet No. 40

Jethro

His doubts weigh insecurely on his mind
as he snarls at every word I speak.
On every task, his words are never kind
but gossip only serves to make him weak.
He whispers lies, and always lingers with
deceit that clearly begs for me to fail;
twisted words take flight in careless myth
while truth stands firm to denigrate his tale.
Still he rages, rarely knowing why
as gadgets with his gimmicks form his shield;
seeking aptness, he can only try
to grip the weapons others firmly wield.
    Jethro schemes but let his fate be shown;
    Like those before him, he will fall alone.

Sonnet No. 41

Chicago

Her skyline stretches wide across the lake;
Streets lie still beneath her tender care
and wishful totes of visions callers stake
discoveries in their futures hiding there.
By day, they marvel in the towers' height
where pen and paper pave ambitious ways;
By evening rhythm brings a new delight
with richness that enlightens greater praise.
Corners hold seductive tales to mark
the river casting hopes since its debut,
and nothing evil lingers in the dark
to mask her promise all will seek as true.
Chicago is a foothold strong and wise
where dreams can rise to meet the midwest skies.

Sonnet No. 42

Golden Gift

A golden halo crafted out of grace;
The only one among us crowned in light
with flickered virtue falling from her face
worn brighter than the stars that fill the night.

A family bread in darkness as we are.
This little girl who sparkles something rare,
a gift of light descended from my star;
The unmistaken answer to my prayer.
She is the flame where shadows used to lie
glistening through lifetime's longest day
while others wonder how and question why:
I remember when I knelt to pray.

My daughter born of sunshine from the start
to hold a place of love within my heart.

Sonnet No. 43

Flight Of The Little Superhero

My little boy with dreams so bold and bright
believes that he can fly beyond the sky;
with every leap of faith he takes his flight,
a flashing ray of light that hustles by.
He strikes his pose with arms outstretched in pride
proclaiming powers for all his world to see;
The universe shall know him far and wide,
his human form is only known to me.
His fearless heart defies all earthly pain,
heroic courage gleaming from his eyes;
each endless mission never shows restrain
his might is greater than his mortal guise.
My child shall lift my spirits ever high;
watching him reminds me how to fly.

Sonnet No. 44

Reflecting Lake

Upon your stillness peaceful dreams reside.
A mirror on the land of my embrace
even when away you're at my side;
A placid haven begging nature's grace.
Your ripples whisper tales of starry nights
where moonbeams dance upon a tranquil face
and as the dawn arises into sight
I hear your gentle waves begin their chase.

Distance draws a veil across your shore;
A barrier of time that rips apart
and in your flux my longing still is pure
for we've been joined together from the start.
    Soon I'll look upon you with delight
    and see my soul reflecting in your light.

Sonnet No. 45

Safe Harbor

Winds smack fiercely on the window pane;
Thunder beckons deeply at the door;
The little ones don't understand the rain
while rushing into bed across the floor.
With trembling lips they snuggle to my ear;
Bolts of lightning widening their eyes;
Their weeps and whimpers illustrate their fear
until they hear their favorite lullabies.

With heads upon my shoulders now they rest
in rhythmic beats the storm begins to fade;
Outside the rage, but here our hearts are blessed;
within our harbor storms cannot invade.
    In the arms of family, tensions break
      and children do not need to stay awake.

Sonnet No. 46

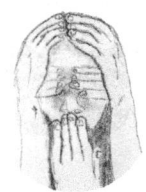

A Step Away

Not by blood but you were reared my son
although you never yearned to call me Dad.
Teach you right from wrong is what I've done
but now we wonder what we ever had.

I rarely hear from you on special days
and only with a task you need to fund;
we know we disagree in many ways
but you should still return and be a son.
Your strongest ties were always to another;
seldom would you ask to hear my news
always you would counsel with the others
because with them you did not have my rules.

In your thoughts I may not be the one,
but I shall always know you as a son.

Sonnet No. 47

Middle Brother

Middle brother, stay a little longer;
Long enough to teach me not to fight.
You didn't even know you made me stronger
or helped me sleep at peace into the night.
You took the hardest hits among us all;
I know they still persist to haunt your mind
perhaps that's why you threw the fastest ball
or how you manage now to be so kind.
The boldest of us you have grown to be;
The bonds that tie your family prove enough
so now, like you, the rest of us can see
that belts and insults did not make us tough.
Between us there will never be another
like you, who grew to be our strongest brother.

Sonnet No. 48

Middle Of The Pool

Others yearned the pool far more than us
but we made good for many righteous reasons
and countless rules of life we did discuss,
even when the swim was out of season.
He often tried to teach me how to swim
but lessons lingered into songs and games;
We laughed until horizon lights grew dim
and wondered if we should have different names.

Those evenings in the pool came crashing down
when half our time together went astray;
Strength could mask the cry but not the frown
and still I cannot swim, to our dismay.

For them, the pool was far too small to think;
For us, it wasn't deep enough to sink.

Sonnet No. 49

Mommy Wasn't Kissing Santa

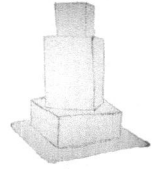

They didn't witness mommy kissing Santa.
Still he laid their presents at the tree
and in the early Christmas morning banter
nothing ostentatious did they see.

Santa did his work before the rise
while children slept, and so did mommy too;
Santa yearned to see their gleaming eyes
while Mrs. Clause prepared her favorite brew.
The morning never went as Santa planned
but children played and never were the wise;
They opened all their presents by their hand
and in their eyes they even showed surprise.

    To Santa, it was never for the kiss;
    Christmas for the children not remiss.

Sonnet No. 50

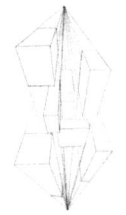

Insomnia

the precise exact algebraic value of pi
is greta garbo visiting or not
and why did robin williams have to die
micheal jordan made his free throw shot
the downstairs bathroom lights might still be on
is socialism really all that bad
and where could all those missing socks have gone
sharon smoked the last cigar I had
hemingway and donne have rung the bell
whooping cranes are very tough to breed
and if we don't confess we go to hell
the mayor didn't get the votes she needs
grandpa died before he told us why ...

the exact precise algebraic value of pi

Sonnet No. 51

My No. 18

You do not compare to Summer's day.
Summer in the plains can never last;
The winds will chase the month of May away
and songs of birds and flowers will have passed.
Both Spring and Autumn grant us greater time
but offer less toward nature's ardent will
and Winter tenders nothing left to rhyme;
Leaving us to ponder further still.
You endure, beginning to the end;
Your spark will shine in sunlight and the shade;
Your hold is soft but never seeks to bend,
Your passion's true and never aims to fade.
    No matter how the sea and clouds may turn
    your love will light your fire's eternal burn.

Sonnet No. 52

Even Playing Field

I dare to comprehend the void of death
through my visions of an aging father.
With my brothers watching his last breath
he slipped away and did not seem to bother.
We rarely harmonized when words were spoken;
I thought him glad the day I drove away;
our truths were neither bent nor fully broken,
rarely was there something left to say.
Our common ground was found around a ball;
Talk of Cooperstown would not recede
to those gaps between us seeming small.
When we spoke of baseball we agreed;
Although he never learned a tender touch
I miss our talk of baseball very much.

Sonnet No. 53

Evening Flower

In youth I chased you with a single glance;
believed our love exploded with my look
as fire ignited inside circumstance.
A touch from you was what it really took.
Time has tempered adolescent's pace
revealing truths that youth had veiled from sight;
no longer swayed by any pleasing face
and knowing passion grows from what is right.

Now I never trust a morning bloom
nor nights that burn without a lasting flame;
a lantern, not a match, should fill the room.
An evening flower is what deserves a name.
Wiser now, I seek a bond that's true
with love that shimmers past the precious few.

Sonnet No. 54

Aristotle's Apostle

The wisdom of a master never dies
but ignorance of students sometimes wins
as pupils often listen to the lies
of promises that ransom friendship's sins.
When blindness drives apostles separate ways
and Aristotle questions what we learn
with every clouded step each actor strays;
the tetrarch grows impatient for returns.
At a peak the teacher takes his hand;
No hesitation casting any blame.
The lone disciple seeks to understand
and wonders if he'll ever shed his shame.
As they resume their journey toward its end
the student knows the tetrarch is his friend.

Sonnet No. 55

Aristotle's Answer

Guidance serves to keep the tetrarch wise
when his pupil's paths and visions stray;
A loyal soul refuses to surprise
even when his students can betray.
Forever close like only chosen few;
A bond as strong as any in the land
and if the teacher must convey his clue
it poses questions solely in her hand.
At the gate she lets the student enter
and bids the tetrarch call again his friend;
His vices past, the student sees the center
showing better judgment in the end.
The lesson learned is obvious to see
as friendship grows into the number three.

Sonnet No. 56

Big Day In The Kitchen

Today my daughter made our family meal.
She brought no caviar nor fine bordeaux
but every bite of every dish was real.
Her presentation turned into a show.
She did forget to use a little salt.
We didn't disapprove the dish or care;
we knew it really wasn't all her fault;
she had a critic propped in every chair.
My little girl soon will be grown up
and she will make her meals for someone new;
He will never drink from Daddy's cup
but he will know her love is just as true
and no meal will ever taste as grand
as a dinner from my daughter's hand.

Sonnet No. 57

A Lawyer's First Day

Early morning, very sharply dressed;
A fresh young lawyer enters the domain;
With eager heart and thundering of chest,
Years of dedication fuel the flame.
Partners pass with looks robust and stern,
Their wisdom showing epoch battles won.
Hallways lined with books and rules to learn;
A gauntlet sets the stage for what's begun.
Conference rooms intense with anxious thought,
Conflicts take their shape in measured phrase;
These are moments law school never taught;
The strength it takes to best a lawyers' gaze;
    and as the day unveils its mystic shroud
      the novice finds the strength to speak aloud.

Sonnet No. 58

Her Second Sonnet

The only one with whom I chose to lay,
to know and love until the end of time.
Alas, I failed to beg that she would stay
when she refused my early words of rhyme;
but yes, she did produce for me an heir
and then saw fit to give to me another.
More love and joy than any man can bare
but she had chosen just to be their mother.

Tears emerged as verse transformed to taunts;
children watched their mother mask her fears
and poets lost the words for what she wants
as she embarked to reconstruct her years;
And so the page with her initial sonnet
ebbed away with nothing left upon it.

Sonnet No. 59

Single Parenting

One child needs a bandage on her finger;
Another wants to know what is for dinner;
They're learning who can be the loudest singer
And fighting over who will be the winner.
The bills piled on the table must be paid;
The kids will need their lunches made for school;
My project due at work cannot be late
And someone overflowed the bathroom stool.
The lightbulb needs replaced above the door;
Grandma's mad we can't return her call;
The dog (I think) just tinkled on the floor
And someone wrote his homework on the wall.
Sometime in support of mental health
I hope to find a moment for myself.

Sonnet No. 60

Our Cabin

We built a cabin on a quiet lake;
It calls us when we start to feel alone.
We used to visit only for a break;
Until we learned it really is our home.

Fishing, swimming, boating all around;
With our favorite culinary treats,
To feed the many friendships we have found,
And strangers we are also glad to greet.

Our cabin now is more than just a drive;
It's cherished as our favorite place to dwell.
A gathering where friends and family thrive;
Where past and present's future bid us well.

Never do we ever care to roam
From the cabin on the lake that we call home.

Sonnet No. 61

When The Music Ends

While in my arms her heart would softly beat
through whispers pure that danced upon the day;
Her unveiled eyes made every moment sweet
and like a fool I let her slip away.
Her laughter fashioned bells of Christmas morning;
a symphony that echoed in my soul
but fearless doubts assumed to give me warning
that vanquished every note and took control.

Now miles away at oceanside she lives;
Her rhythm fills the joy in other's care;
Her voice still shines in everything she gives
but in her song is nothing we can share.
She is gone and all that's left to see
are melodies no longer meant for me.

Sonnet No. 62

The Artisan

With colors bright, you paint your world new,
each stroke constructs the artist who you are;
every thought and inspiration true,
your canvas christened by a guiding star.
You draft an opus on your sacred scroll
not in vain, but from a naked light
you tire as your epoch takes its toll
but gently still you vest in sounding sight.
Images form mirrors into your soul
reflecting all your inner strength and pride
with every part, you shape the perfect whole;
A masterpiece to let your faith reside.
Cast your dreams and let them touch the sky
through your craft, your wings will surely fly.

Sonnet No. 63

New Beginning

Two banks sought to merge and grow as one,
Divergent paths conjoined to form a stride;
The journey's perseverance finally won,
When courage steered each ship against its tide.

Different teams assemble in their course,
A fresh beginning pushes them anew.
Their leaders form a stable guiding force,
With futures bright in optimistic view.

Their walls grow strong like pillars in the field,
Firmly placed by able trusted hands;
They count the costs but never do they yield
As their banner hoists above the lands.

Evolution of this voyage has ensured
That life and growth around them will endure.

Sonnet No. 64

Peoria

Her rolling hills will lead you from the river
to sprawling plains into the harvests' yields
where winter fires protect you from the shiver
while children wait to play in summer's fields.
The author of our atlas must have known
this axis gathers souls from every strand;
as varied generations who have grown
will rise again to reap this fertile land.
Those who come to wonder of her age
and levitate to walk the hollowed ground
can learn to understand her vital stage
and see where opportunities are found.
If you pursue a true midwestern dream,
explore this splendid city by the stream.

Sonnet No. 65

Stronger Than He Knows

He is the one sincere within his boast
of boundless speed and arms outstretched to soar.
Skipping rooms as if from coast to coast;
his laughter now is louder than his roar.
Revealing that he needs his soul to grow;
believing that his future shakes the ground;
and in his eyes the world around him knows
in every day another dream is found.

His makeshift cape is gone without a trace;
Reality has dampened varied cheers
but villains ever cower from his chase
even as his profile shows the years.
His power may not fight as many foes
but now he's even stronger than he knows.

Sonnet No. 66

Starlit Lily

She was like a loving starlit lily
spreading pollen no one else could find;
even when I acted rather silly
she smiled as if she didn't really mind.
She kissed me when I wanted it to be
and wandered when I should be left alone;
She rested when I needed to be free,
encouraged me when facing the unknown.
She wrote me letters that I feared to read;
Her jealousy was sometimes not to bare;
Stubbornly she knew we should succeed
so I lied to her, and said I didn't care.

Today she shares her pollen with another
and I wish we could still be with each other.

Sonnet No. 67

Lanny Trent

The world knows your story, Lanny Trent
or at least the special versions that you tell.
They see the mounds of money that you've spent
and envy all the places where you dwell.
Once you were a brother next to me
for many years we fabricated plans;
the two of us together soon to be
foremost among the leaders of our land.
Then I wasn't good enough for you;
you angled off with others by your side.
Neither of us knew what I would do
but I would not be with you for your ride.
    The crowd around you marvels at your fame
    but I am one who understands your name.

Sonnet No. 68

Guardian Angel On Overtime

Once before my life did almost end
but a savior rose to cast Azrael away.
This second time I cannot comprehend
what transpired to keep me from harm's way:
highway traffic stopped with me in line;
the busy folks behind me didn't see;
the catastrophic crash came from behind.
I walked away, but not that family.

Time can stop when riddles smack your face
reminding you of promises undone;
hoping prayers will send you to the place
where everlasting peace can still be won.
    Today again was not my day to die;
    unlike before, I wake to wonder why.

Sonnet No. 69

Noises At The Door

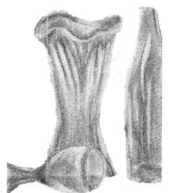

Did you hear those noises at the door
returning in the early hours of dawn;
the pounding of the heals upon the floor
breathing soft until the sounds were gone?
Did you know the nature of the clamor
and who engaged the night so brazenly;
why the speech was shrouded in a stammer
while nothing in the voice gave clarity?

The worst of nights would escalate from there
when lights came on anxiety would grow
extending more than anyone should bare.

Please tell me, children, that you didn't know.

As time decays, perhaps we should explore
the nature of those noises at the door.

Sonnet No. 70

Contradictions
In The Controversy

Before the wine could reach its crowning sip
the bandage broke and beckoned me to bleed.
The only time the botox on her lips
admitted her misdeeds as I perceived.

Never was my future so unclear.
All that's left to do would seem undone;
at least my children always would be near
and they could point me toward a healing sun.

As foretold, the fault declared was mine
but I stood solemn in my toxic mirror
as she embarked a path that would unwind
and take her to a place inside her fear.
Clouded is the way we all must go
to face a path that only God can know.

Sonnet No. 71

Miss You, Sister

Platonic thoughts between us not remiss,
for nothing in our blood could cause a stir
but ways that we would talk and reminisce
made special siblings of the friends we were.
You walked into my life a great surprise;
I never thought to gain such fortune's send
a sister who I thought would never rise
and bring a voice of reason to my end.

Our journey did not last as we had planned;
another joined our path and wouldn't see
no need for petty jealousy at hand
but blame was never yours; it was me.
Now the other is no longer here
but I still fear we may not persevere.

Sonnet No. 72

Birthday Wish

Today you all forgot my day of birth.
Now I know this feeling all alone
to question years of sinew and self-worth
and logarithms failing in my bones;
Hoping for a call or text by phone;
Praying for arrival of some mail;
Maybe just a note tied to a stone;
Something to foretell a different tale.

Shed a tear in shame, I shall not do;
Relationships in transit will proceed
as sympathy and shame will not pursue
my family's complexity that bleeds.
Still this day, I wish they were aware
and they were here instead of over there.

Sonnet No. 73

Hypocritical Oath

Upon admission solemn words were spoken
to guard the Constitution that we teach
with rules of ethics never to be broken;
but conflicts soon arise as plans beseech
within the jurisprudence there lies sin
when justice bends to well-intentioned aims
to understand the game is played to win
where right and wrong give way to stated claims.

Ambition can compel a path to tread
while pride demands what victory belies;
legal tools of trade that sever heads
may mock the oath when ancient splendor dies.
The price is paid with righteousness insane
as endless justice battlefields remain.

Sonnet No. 74

Crossroads

Lovers often see their end in sight
where they can glimpse their finish of forever;
should one turn left, the other take a right
or hold each others' hands and walk together?
If one seeks a fire, their flames will part;
If one still needs a purpose they will stray;
If either thinks they need a novel start
their story may not last another day.
If they choose to take each others' hands
and count their costs and blessings all at once,
their long-ago may not outweigh their plans
and let them conquer questions they confront.
    One can cause a union's end in shame
    but two can build a dynasty to claim.

Sonnet No. 75

Darkest Times

My therapist asks of thoughts to end my life.
Submerged with chilled emotions that I hide,
my narrative cuts through without a knife
and to my trusted counselor I have lied.
Truths immerse in lies from sordid years
as the gun laid on my desk stares back at me,
with no one near to comfort falling tears
or elevate the man I need to be.

St. Thomas the Apostle steers the way
as faith in Jesus Christ is fighting through.
A call reveals signs of stark and gray
and children at my side will help me, too.

Know the tools that could abet my crimes
stay locked away amidst these darkest times.

Sonnet No. 76

Redemption's Price

Leadership is nice, but twice then thrice
can draw a price that leads to bitter blood.
Each choice will need a sacrifice
to paddle through an unexpected flood;
Divergence turns on currents in a gale
where ground beneath the water often quakes;
Neverending risks the task might fail
revealing what will reap if valor breaks.

Into port redemption comes with haze;
Its essence fuels a solace in the fight
when even on the worst of lonesome days
a leader must commit to what is right.
Though doubt will linger where a captain stands,
the heart will know to always guide the hands.

Sonnet No. 77

Where Art Thou, Thou Art Here

My neighbor asks if God is here today.
I hesitate, unknowing where he's been.
I should bid my brother kneel and pray
but rather, ask how this one I might win.
The Book tells us to walk and spread the Word
but I respond that all of us are saved.
Am I like Peter waiting for the third
or Judas on a path already paved?

Then I recall the wage of sin is death;
accept, believe, confess is our release;
and He will know upon our final breath
if we receive His ever lasting peace.
When in fear and facing hidden tests,
the Words of Jesus echo at their best.

Sonnet No. 78

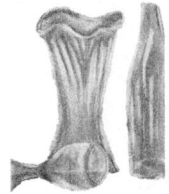

More Than Twelve Steps Away

I wish someone had listened to my plea
when I was still a shadow standing near,
but laden chains that no one else could see
have darkened idle hopes that once were dear.
A demon's grip has taken very tight
to sully light that once was in the eyes,
with little might to travel through the night
or strength to part the courage from the lies.

Pray for will to walk in better ways
and find the peace of mind that must have fled;
return unto a bed where virtue lays
but find it now before someone is dead.
Faith and hope must teach what we can gain
so all of us can move beyond the pain.

Sonnet No. 79

Seeking Dissolution

Another note to read from her attorney.
Hoping it might stop this endless stress;
for several years I've ventured on this journey,
tried to cease the catastrophic mess
but nothing in her words brings clarity
nor demonstrates a manifest intent;
so onward flows the same disparity
in unrestrained pursuit of some content.

Now we travel toward another year.
The costs and fees of nullities will mount
but still with no conclusion drawing near
and fading assets left for us to count.
Once I saw this as a righteous test,
now it only makes me more depressed.

Sonnet No. 80

Consequences Earned

This empty bedroom knows regrets too well
as silence holds the stillness crowding light;
the battles that my demons often tell
were those preserved by darkness in the nights.
This path was not among the ones I chose
as now in separate places we reside,
while love's deceit refuses to disclose
how saints can lose where raging anger hides.
Hold close the truths that we may someday find
with dignity behind us as we learn
some stories are the type to leave behind
but also carry consequences earned.
    Now I fight alone to struggle through
    the lessons that disclose what I must do.

Sonnet No. 81

New Year's Resolution

(Akitu)

The reasons why we honor New Year's Day:
perhaps for Carl's grass or Edna's spring
to honor Bryant's verse or Jackson's sway
or maybe Burns who wanted us to sing.
By any script it's not a solemn moment
nor should it be a fleeting point in time,
when all our poets lead us to atonement
and dignify romance through subtle rhyme.
Some should want to spend the day in prayer
and others will refuse to call it blessed;
Pessimists suggest we should beware
while pioneers begin their newest quest.
In Babylon, they celebrated right;
they used the day to see their futures bright.

Sonnet No. 82

Magic Words

Doubters question logic in the magic.
Skeptics argue whether God exists.
To deny them both would be an act so tragic
even for our wisest scientists.
Neither can be held inside the hand
nor be consumed like finely cooked cuisine,
but inside every parcel through the land
lies their hidden tangibles unseen.
Know that faith and magic fill the hour
every time the syllables are spoken
on command to summon all the power
nothing in our world has ever broken.
For those who seek to use the magic words,
"I love you, Dad" is all that need be heard.

Sonnet No. 83

Remembering You

Sometimes I still feel a heart that beats
like angels' voices only dreamers hear;
in my mind your eyes do not retreat
so now I wonder why you're never near.
Do memories have an expiration date?

The only thing you did to lead us wrong
was love me in a way that tested fate
and sing to me an uninvited song.
You told me I was apt at many things;
so why was I so ignorant in this
forsaking all the gifts that you could bring
and turning from the love that I would miss?
I still cannot surmise the reasons why
I never tried to say the right goodbye.

Sonnet No. 84

The Person I Should Be

The one before you walked away from me.
The vows she spoke outgrew their usefulness;
she recognized she wanted to be free
while disregarding answers to confess.
Forgive me if at first I cannot find
the fortunes she and I once sought together;
what she covets struck me from behind
so you must help recapture my forever.

I know her destiny was laid astray
to clear a space inside that I once knew;
that you are not the kind to step away
and I will never turn away from you.
Please find patience left inside of me
and help release the person I should be.

Sonnet No. 85

My Own Private Sisyphus

Who rolled the weighted boulder up the hill?
Was it Hercules, Perseus, or someone else more recent?
Did the mountain move or was it standing still?
Was he a hero, or slightly more indecent?

Our myths are often grounded in some truth;
we try to learn the burdens that they bore
as decades pass and we exhume our youth
the fates refuse to serve us anymore.
Our knowledge lends to wisdom as a gift
while faith and courage join us if we choose;
these tools converge to guide us through our rift
and help to overcome the will of fools.
Remember when the boulders test our bones
we never really climb our hills alone.

Sonnet No. 86

Look Starboard

The voyage of life brings tides of time that shift
and those who stay aboard are hard to find.
Torrid storms can carry oars adrift
but bows and sterns are always intertwined.
Horizons fade and sunlight turns to gray
but loyalty builds a lighthouse through it all;
no distance - nor the ocean's great dismay -
can desolate a mast that stretches tall.

Leaks and reinforcements tread as one
when trust and honor form the common base;
no need for words when action must be done,
faith leads shipmates to their destined place.
Friends in life forever growing old
persevere through all that may unfold.

Sonnet No. 87

Do You Think Of Me?

Did you think of me at all today?
Do you remember any funny quirks,
or when we met for lunch and didn't pay
and are you still amazed by fireworks?
Only you could see inside the charm
and grasp the depth that lurked behind the face
and know that warmth can rise above the harm
and life's dilemmas should not cause disgrace.
But now there's so much else to think about;
I admit my thoughts have wandered, too;
still I wonder if you have your doubts
that I will find the time to think of you.
    The next time that I send a thought your way
    remember me and have a joyous day.

Sonnet No. 88

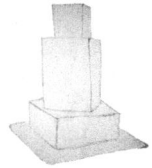

Clean Bedrooms

Why won't children stop to clean their rooms?
The question is a simple one to ask;
if left alone they will become a tomb
consuming for an adolescent task;
much too busy playing childish games
or entertaining classmates on their phones,
assigning to themselves creative names
exaggerating how much they have grown.
Eventually the door slams in my face.
The grunge has grown beyond a simple mop;
yet they declare this is their sacred space
and maybe it is me who needs to stop.

Never mind, I dread the coming dawn
and spotless rooms revealing they have gone.

Sonnet No. 89

Moving Into Her Boyfriend's Apartment

A home is not a place that's bought or sold
or bricks surrounding front doors and a back;
its quarters will embrace both young and old
and everyone's delusions stay intact.
A home is not a place to turn away
or routine stop to share your salutations;
nor does it only thrive on Holidays
or serve for only special celebrations.
Your home will never cast your visions out
or shame you when you cannot pay the rent;
there's always something new to talk about
and you'll return no matter where you went.
Your home is in your values, thoughts, and spirit,
and knowing that your heart is always near it.

Sonnet No. 90

We Will Know

In dreams I've sketched your face so many times
and whispers in the night have brought you near;
though still unseen you send to me your signs
in melodies that only I can hear.
Your laughter in the dawn awakes my day,
You touch me with a breeze upon my skin;
Unspoken words between us try to say
when the space between us will give in.
Someday we will seize the stars above
and journey to our destiny's embrace;
we will never need to prove our love
after we have overcome our chase.
When we meet my heart will know it's you,
and yours will know that you have found me, too.

Sonnet No. 91

A Prayer For The One I Find Most Difficult

Lord, please hear my ever sinful plea
For one so far away but could be near;
Whose soul is bound by chains we cannot see
With warmth that's lost and darkened into fear.
An evil grip is stretching very tight;
It shades the light once shining in the eyes
But You, O Lord, can guide them through the plight
And turn them toward a path where truth replies.
Restore the strength to walk a humble way,
Let peace and love replace the evil swagger;
And for my selfish thoughts as I do pray
Please steady my assumptions as they stagger.
Grant us strength to rise above our needs
And carry out Your Will through living deeds.

Sonnet No. 92

To Walk Alone

I've never been a man with many friends
as I submerge them to my definition;
once subscribed I keep it to the end
until we reach our separate perdition.
This brotherhood we rarely talk about;
different paths but never parting ways,
forever faithful even when in doubt
and always leaning toward our future days.
We follow different callings in our plan,
nostalgic pasts but vastly different means
in serving selves but also fellow man
while sometimes neverending where we seem.
Always near is friendship lasting true
right behind the tests that we pursue.

Sonnet No. 93

Son Of Mine

You're the one God sent to look like me,
And carry on the mantle of our name;
Both good and bad for history to see;
Though your future does not look the same.

They liken us in times it is unfair;
Quicker you will always seem to run;
Ambitions rise with conquests to declare;
As puzzles of your destiny are spun.

Ironic it may be to gaze at you;
And wonder for tomorrow's wants and needs;
Chronicle the good and bad you do,
And hope that I will count among your deeds.

Know your path, to end and from the start,
Shall always travel deep inside my heart.

Sonnet No. 94

Always My Princess

You were sent in answer to my Prayer;
All the nights I walked beneath that star,
And promised every twilight it was there,
That you and I would never drift afar.

You journeyed to me just as I had asked,
But different as the day engulfs the night.
You brought a future to my clouded past,
And from the shadows I could sense your light.

You were the first, but cast into a riddle,
Begging questions from your chosen distance,
That never let you realize in the middle,
You would be my one and only Princess.

And every evening, whether near or far,
I look upon and thank that splendid star.

Sonnet No. 95

The Deep End

For several weeks we followed every rule.
The world's pandemic had to run its course;
she smiled and bid me sit next to the pool
and told me it was time for a divorce.
The children didn't factor in for her
to cradle all the promises she made;
our years together ending a blur,
the dreams we framed had suddenly decayed.
I left the pool as stagnant water dried
and burdens fell on me so she could stay.
I was labelled selfish with the tide,
hypocrisy engulfed the game we played.
While in my shattered solitude of time
I set these many memories to rhyme.

Epilogue

Not Dead Yet

Many of my words still locked away
but I admit the thoughts within me dwell,
and I have lifted reasons left to stay
with no intentions lurking back to hell.
Often life's debates lie in myself
to stifle futures cast into a doubt,
but now I have a Book upon my shelf
to help me learn what life should be about.
Demons need to bring their biggest gun;
fights with me will dive a deeper plunge.
When they come again, I will not run
and they will learn the power of my punch.

Despite their menace, I am far from dead
and I believe my best days lie ahead.

Author Bio

AJ Streator is a compelling storyteller who crafts narratives that transport readers to new worlds and challenges their intellectual perspectives. With a background in law and language arts, his education and passion for human stories enables AJ to bring depth, humanity, and authenticity to every tale.

Drawing from years of professional experience, AJ understands the power of poetry and story to educate, inspire, and connect people across different cultures and experiences.

When not writing, AJ can be found exploring new places, engaging with readers, annoying his family, and continually honing his philosophy and behavior toward the world around us.

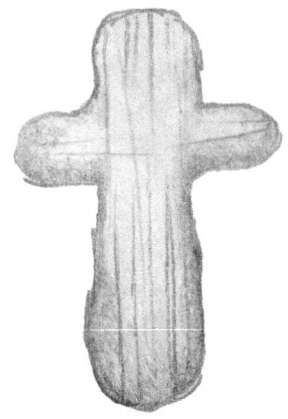

"While in my shattered solitude of time
I set these many memories to rhyme."

AJ Streator

Made in the USA
Monee, IL
31 December 2025